Anonymous

Metropolitan coin book

Containing accurate engravings of the various gold, silver and other coins

Anonymous

Metropolitan coin book
Containing accurate engravings of the various gold, silver and other coins

ISBN/EAN: 9783337223465

Printed in Europe, USA, Canada, Australia, Japan

Cover: Foto ©Andreas Hilbeck / pixelio.de

More available books at **www.hansebooks.com**

(PRICE TWENTY-FIVE CENTS.)

METROPOLITAN COIN BOOK,

CONTAINING ACCURATE ENGRAVINGS OF

The various Gold, Silver and other Coins now in Circulation throughout the World;

ARRANGED IN THEIR PROPER ORDER OF VALUE,

AND UNDER THE HEAD OF THE RESPECTIVE GOVERNMENTS BY WHICH THEY ARE ISSUED;

TOGETHER WITH

A COMPLETE INDEX,

BY THE AID OF WHICH THE COINS OF EVERY NATION CAN BE FOUND AT A GLANCE, AND THE

UNITED STATES MINT VALUE OF EACH ASCERTAINED.

The Metropolitan Bank Note Reporter and Bank Register

IS FURNISHED TO SUBSCRIBERS AT THE FOLLOWING PRICES:

TO CITY SUBSCRIBERS.			TO MAIL SUBSCRIBERS.	
Weekly,	by Carrier, ...$3 00 per an.	Weekly,.... ....$2 75 per an.
Semi-monthly,	" .... 2 00 "	Semi-monthly,................. ..... 1 75 "
Monthly.	" .... 1 25 "	Monthly,..................... .... 1 25 "

THE REPORTER IS CORRECTED BY THE

METROPOLITAN BANK and Messrs. GWYNNE & DAY, 21 Wall St., cor. Broad.

TO EACH SUBSCRIBER FOR ANY EDITION WHO PAYS ONE YEAR IN ADVANCE, A COPY OF THIS COIN BOOK WILL BE GIVEN

GRATIS.

THE DESCRIPTIVE REGISTER

OF GENUINE BANK NOTES

Is published at 75 cents, and furnished to all subscribers to the Reporter, who pay one year in advance, *gratis.*

New York:

PUBLISHED BY THE PROPRIETORS OF THE
METROPOLITAN BANK NOTE REPORTER AND BANK REGISTER.
1865.

METROPOLITAN COIN BOOK,

CONTAINING ACCURATE ENGRAVINGS OF

The various Gold, Silver and other Coins now in Circulation throughout the World;

ARRANGED IN THEIR PROPER ORDER OF VALUE,

AND UNDER THE HEAD OF THE RESPECTIVE GOVERNMENTS BY WHICH THEY ARE ISSUED;

TOGETHER WITH

A COMPLETE INDEX,

BY THE AID OF WHICH THE COINS OF EVERY NATION CAN BE FOUND AT A GLANCE, AND THE UNITED STATES MINT VALUE OF EACH ASCERTAINED.

The Metropolitan Bank Note Reporter and Bank Register

IS FURNISHED TO SUBSCRIBERS AT THE FOLLOWING PRICES:

TO CITY SUBSCRIBERS.				TO MAIL SUBSCRIBERS.	
Weekly,	by Carrier,	$3 00 per an.	Weekly,	$2 75 per an.	
Semi-monthly,	"	2 00 "	Semi-monthly,	1 75 "	
Monthly,		1 25 "	Monthly,	1 25 "	

THE REPORTER IS CORRECTED BY THE

METROPOLITAN BANK and Messrs. GWYNNE & DAY, 21 Wall St., cor. Broad.

TO EACH SUBSCRIBER FOR ANY EDITION WHO PAYS ONE YEAR IN ADVANCE, A COPY OF THIS COIN BOOK WILL BE GIVEN

GRATIS.

THE DESCRIPTIVE REGISTER

OF GENUINE BANK NOTES

Is published at 75 cents, and furnished to all subscribers to the Reporter, who pay one year in advance, *gratis.*

New York:

PUBLISHED BY THE PROPRIETORS OF THE

METROPOLITAN BANK NOTE REPORTER AND BANK REGISTER.

1865.

INDEX

TO

METROPOLITAN COIN BOOK,

WITH THE

UNITED STATES MINT VALUE OF EACH COIN.

CJ1753
-M5

31

GOLD COINS OF THE UNITED STATES.	Dollars	Cents	Page
Quintuple Eagle	50.00		5
Double Eagle	20.00		5
California 2½ Eagle	23.50		5
" Double Eagle	19.90		5
" " "	19.20		5
" " "	16.00		5
Old Eagle (1795)	18.50		5
Eagle, (1841)	10.00		5
Cincinnati Mining Co.'s Eagle	9.00		5
Humbert's California Eagle	9.90		5
J. S. O. " "	9.85		5
Moffatt's " "	9.85		6
Templeton's " "	9.85		6
Miners' Bank " "	9.85		6
Mormon Piece	8.00		6
Oregon Co., (Beaver Coin)	8.00		6
Old Half Eagle	5.25		6
Half Eagle	5.00		6
Mass. Calif'a Comp'y ½ Eagle	4.75		6
Bechtler Half Eagle	4.75		6
Dunbar & Co. Calif'a ½ Eagle	4.75		6
N. G. & N. San Francisco ½ Eagle	4.85		6
California Half Eagle	4.55		6
Oregon Comp'y "	4.75		6
Three-dollar Piece	3.00		6
Old Quarter Eagle	2.62		6
Mormon Piece	4.00		6
Quarter Eagle	2.50		6
Georgia ¼ Eagle	2.37		6
North Carolina Dollar	.93		6
Bechtler Dollar	.93		6
Old One-dollar Piece	1.00		6
New " " "	1.00		6
California Half Dollar	.40		6
" Quarter Dollar	.20		6

SILVER COINS OF THE UNITED STATES.			
Pine-tree Shilling	.16		6
Quarter Dollar	.25		6
Dollars	1.00		7
Half Dollar	.56		7
Dime	.10		7
Half Dime	.05		7

PLATINA, COPPER, & NICKEL COINS OF THE UNITED STATES.			
Three-cent Piece, (Platina)	.03		7
One " " (Copper)	.01		7
One " " (Nickel)	.01		7

GOLD AND SILVER COINS OF MEXICO.			
Doubloon, (Gold)	15.45		8
Dollars, (Silver)	1.04		8
Half Dollar, "	.50		8
Quarter Dollar, "	.25		8
Real, "	.12		8
Half Real, "	.06		8
Quarter Real, "	.03		8

GOLD COINS OF SOUTH & CENTRAL AMERICA.	Dollars	Cents	Page
Old Doubloon	15.50		8
Doubloons	15.50		8
Doubloons	15.50		9
Half Doubloon	7.75		9
Bogota Doubloon	15.25		9
Half Doubloon	7.75		9
Moidore	6.00		9
Half Joe of Brazil	6.00		9
" " "	8.50		9
Moidore "	4.75		9
Quarter Doubloon	3.67		9
Pistole	3.75		9
Half Pistole	1.87		9
Half Pistole	1.75		9
Half Doubloon	1.90		9
Quarter Pistole	.90		9
Quarter Pistole	.87		9
Quarter Pistole, (Brazil)	.60		9

SILVER COINS OF SOUTH & CENTRAL AMERICA.			
Piece of 1200 Reis	1.00		10
" 960 Reis	1.00		10
Eight Reals	1.00		10
Eight Reals	.97		11
Eight Reals, (Bolivia)	1.05		11
Eight Reals, (Grenada)	.96		11
Patagon	.90		11
Eight Reals, (base)	.60		11
Four Reals	.50		11
Four Reals, (Argentine)	.45		11
Four Reals, (Peru)	.45		11
Four Reals, (base)	.33		11
Piece of 300 Reis	.25		11
Real	.11		11
Real, (base)	.07		11
Four Reals	.44		12
Four Reals, (base)	.34		12
Four Reals, (base)	.33		12
Two Reals	.20		12
Two Reals, (base)	.16		12
Two Reals, (base)	.15		12
Real	.11		12
Real	.10		13
Real, (base)	.08		13
Real, (base)	.05		13
Half Real, (base)	.04		13

GOLD COINS OF GREAT BRITAIN.			
Five Sovereigns	24.10		13
Double Sovereign	9.64		13
Mohur	6.72		13
Guinea	5.00		13
Sovereign	4.82		13
Half Guinea	2.50		13
Half Sovereign	2.40		13
Half Sovereign	2.30		13
One-third Guinea	1.66		13

SILVER COINS OF GREAT BRITAIN.	Dollars	Cents	Page
William III. Crown	1.10		14
Queen Anne Crown	1.10		14
George III. Crown	1.10		14
Victoria Crown	1.10		14
Charles II. Crown	1.10		14
Bank of Ireland Token	1.00		14
Crown	1.00		14
Bank of England Token	1.00		14
William and Mary ½ Crown	.55		14
Queen Anne ½ Crown	.55		14
George IV. ½ Crown	.55		15
Charles II. ½ Crown	.55		15
George III. ½ Crown	.55		15
Three Shilling Token	.50		15
Thirty-penny Token	.40		15
John Robertson Token	.40		15
Victoria Florin	.45		15
One-and-sixpenny Token	.22		15
One Shilling	.22		15
Queen Elizabeth Sixpence	.11		15
Sixpence	.11		15
Fourpence	.07		16
Sixpenny Token	.06		16
Threepenny Piece	.05		16
Twopenny Piece	.03		16
One-and-a-halfpenny Piece	.02		16
Onepenny Piece	.02		16

COLONIAL SILVER COINS OF GREAT BRITAIN.			
One Dollar, (Sierra Leone)	.80		16
Three Gilders, (Demerara)	.73		16
Rupee	.40		16
Quarter Pagoda	.34		16
Quarter Dollar	.22		16
Half Rupee	.20		16
Shilling	.22		16
Two Macutos	.20		16
Half Gilder	.12		16
One-eighth Dollar	.11		16
Quarter Rupee	.10		16
Quarter Gilder	.06		16
Two Annas	.05		16
One-sixteenth Dollar	.05		16
One-eighth Gilder	.03		16

SILVER COINS OF CANADA.			
Twenty-cent Piece	.20		44
Ten-cent Piece	.10		44
Five-cent Piece	.05		44

GOLD COINS OF FRANCE.			
Double Louis D'Or	.09		17
Forty Francs	7.64		17
Louis D'Or	4.50		17
Twenty Francs	3.82		17
Ten Francs	1.88		17
Six Francs	1.10		17

SILVER COINS OF ITALY.

Coin	Value	Page
Ten Livres of Tuscany	1.50	35
Sardinian Scudo	1.25	35
Ten Pauls of Tuscany	.95	35
Roman Crown	.95	35
Roman Scudo	.95	35
Crown of Bologna	.95	35
Venetian Scudo	.95	36
Roman Scudo	.95	36
Sicilian Scudo	.90	36
Scudo	.90	36
Five Lire, (Lombardy)	.90	36
Five Livres	.90	36
Five Francs	.90	37
Neapolitan Scudo	.84	37
Neapolitan Ducat	.72	37
Five Drachmi, (Greece)	.78	37
Five Pauls	.44	37
Fifty Grani	.36	37
Two Livres	.35	37
Half Scudo, (base)	.28	37
Half Scudo	.45	37
Half Scudo	.28	37
Roman Testoon	.28	37
Two Lire of Sicily	.35	37
Two Lire of Sicily	.35	38
Roman Testoon	.28	38
Two Pauls	.18	38
Florin	.16	38
Lira	.18	38
One-fifth Scudo of Lucca	.18	38
Sicilian Lira	.16	38
Franc	.16	38
Livre	.16	38
Drachmi, (Greece)	.15	38
Twenty Grani	.15	38
Two Carlini	.15	38
Half Testoon	.14	38
Half Drachmi, (Greece)	.07	38
Ten Soldi	.07	38
Quarter Testoon	.07	38
Fifty Centimes	.07	38
Ten Grani	.06	38
Carlin	.06	39
Seven Soldi	.05	38
Five Soldi	.04	39

SILVER AND GOLD COINS OF SWEDEN, DENMARK & NORWAY,

Coin	Value	Page
Eight Marks	1.10	38
Specie Dollar	.98	38

SILVER AND GOLD COINS OF SWEDEN, DENMARK & NORWAY.

Coin	Value	Page
Rix-dollar	.98	38
Specie Dollar	.98	39
Old Ducatoon	.00	39
Six Marks, (old piece)	.73	39
Forty Schillings	.60	39
Four Marks	.48	39
Half Rix-dollar	.48	39
Half Specie Dollar	.44	39
One-fifth Specie Dollar, (base)	.20	39
One-fourth Specie Dollar	.20	39
Sixteen Skillings, (base)	.10	39
Twenty-four Skillings	.10	39
Twelve Skillings, (base)	.10	39
Twenty Skillings	.05	39
Double Ducat	4.40	40
Eight Skillings	.08	40
Twenty-four Skillings, (base)	.06	40
Two Skillings, (base)	.04	40
Twelve Skillings	.05	40
Eight Danish Skillings	.04	40
Eight Skillings	.03	40
Four Skillings	.02	40
Two Skillings	.01	40

SILVER COINS OF THE NETHERLANDS & HOLLAND.

Coin	Value	Page
Silver Lion	.98	40
Three Gilders	1.06	40
Old Rix-dollar	.98	40
Sixty Stivers	.98	40
Crown of Zurich	.98	40
Specie Dollar	.98	40
Ducatoon	.90	40
Rix-dollar	.90	40
Two-third Rix-dollar	.60	40
Thirty Stivers	.56	40
Specie Dollar	.98	41
Rix-dollar	.00	41
Thirty Stivers	.56	41
Half Rix-dollar	.38	41
Two-thirds Thaler	.43	41
Gilder	.34	41
Gilder	.30	41
Ten Stivers	.18	41
One-sixth Rix-dollar	.15	41
Six Stivers	.09	41
Five Stivers	.08	41
Eight Stivers, (base)	.06	41

SILVER COINS OF THE NETHERLANDS & HOLLAND.

Coin	Value	Page
Six Stivers	.06	41
Half-Rix-dollar	.42	43
Quarter Florin	.10	43
Two Stivers	.03	41

GOLD AND SILVER COINS OF RUSSIA AND POLAND.

Coin	Value	Page
Imperial	4.00	42
Five Roubles	3.95	42
Five Roubles	3.90	42
Rouble-and-a-Half	1.07	42
Rouble	.78	42
Five Zlot	.50	42
Five Zlot	.48	42
Half Rouble	.35	42
Half Rouble	.34	42
Thirty Kopeks	.18	42
Two Zlot	.18	42
Twenty-five Kopeks	.13	42
Twenty Kopeks	.10	42
One Zlot	.10	42
Ten Kopeks	.05	42
Five Kopeks	.03	42

SILVER AND GOLD COINS OF TURKEY.

Coin	Value	Page
Twenty Piastres	.86	43
Five Drachmi	.80	43
Utchilk	.10	43
Half Altilik	.10	43
Altmichlik	.05	43
Piastre	.04	43
Half Drachm	.08	43
Twenty Drachmi	4.40	43

SILVER COINS OF HAYTI.

Coin	Value	Page
One-hundred Cents	.00	43
Twenty-five Cents	.00	43
Twelve Cents	.00	43

TRIPOLITAN & JEWISH COINS.

Coin	Value	Page
Ghersh of Tripoli	.10	43
Fifteen-cent Piece	.15	43
Three-cent Piece	.03	43

METROPOLITAN
COMPLETE COIN BOOK.

CONTAINING

PERFECT FAC-SIMILES

OF ALL THE VARIOUS

Gold, Silver, and other Metallic Coins throughout the World,

WITH THE PRESENT

UNITED STATES MINT VALUE OF EACH COIN UNDER IT.

GOLD COINS OF THE UNITED STATES, AND PRIVATE COIN AGE OF GEORGIA, CALIFORNIA, UTAH, ETC.

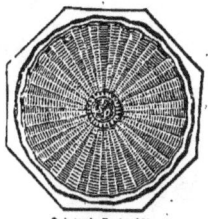

Quintuple Eagle, $50.

Quintuple Eagle, $50.

Double Eagle, $20.

California, 2½ Eagle, $25.50.

California Double Eagle, $19.20.

California Double Eagle, $19.50.

Double Eagle, $16.

Old Eagle, $10.50.

Old Eagle, 10.50.

Eagle, $9.60.

Eagle, $9.9.

Eagle, $10.

California Eagle, $9.90.

$9.85.

GOLD COINS OF THE UNITED STATES.

California Eagle, $9.65.   California Eagle, $9.35.   Eagle, $9.65.

Eagle, $9.65.   Mormon, $8. $6.   Old ½ Eagle, $5.25.   Old ½ Eagle, $5.25.

Old ½ Eagle, $5.25.   Old ½ Eagle, $5.25.   ½ Eagle, $5.   ½ Eagle, $5. $4.75. $4.75.

California Half Eagle, $4.75. $4.35. $4.65. $4.65. $4.65.

$4.75. $4.75. $3. $4.   Old ½ Eagle, $2.62   Old ½ Eagle, $2.62

Mormon, $4.   ½ Eagle, $2.50   ½ Eagle, $2.50.   Georgia ½ Eagle, $2.37.   New, $1.

$1 $1.   North Carolina Dollar, 93 cts.   28C   California ½ Dollar, 40 cts.   California ¼ Dollar, 20 cts.

SILVER COINS OF THE UNITED STATES.

Pine-tree shilling, 10 cts.   ½ Dollar, 25 cts.   ½ Dollar, 25 cts.

SILVER COINS OF THE UNITED STATES—*Continued.*

Dollar, $1.

Dollar, $1.

Dollar, $1.

Dollar, $1.

Dime, 10 cts.

Dollar $1.

Dollar, $1

Dollar, $1.

Dime, 10 cts.

½ Dollar, 50 cts.

½ Dollar, 50 cts.

½ Dollar, 50 cts.

½ Dollar, 50 cts.

½ Dollar, 50 cts.

½ Dollar 50 cts.

¼ Dollar, 25 cts.

½ Dime, 5 cts.

½ Dime, 5 cts.

¼ Dollar, 25 cts.

¼ Dollar, 25 cts.

Dime, 10 cts.

Dime, 10 cts.

Dime, 10 cts.

Dime, 10 cts.

½ Dime, 5 cts.

COPPER AND NICKEL COINS OF THE UNITED STATES.

3 cts.   New Nickel, 1 ct.   Old Copper, 1 cent.   Nickel, 1 cent.   3 cts.

GOLD AND SILVER COINS OF MEXICO.

Doubloon, $15.45.   Dollar, $1.04.   Dollar, $1.04.   Dollar $1.04.

½ Dollar, 50 cts.   Dollar, $1.04.   Dollar, $1.04.   ¼ Dollar, 50 cts.

Real, 12 cts.   ¼ Dollar, 25 cts.   ¼ Dollar, 25 cts.   ¼ Dollar, 25 cts.   ¼ Dollar, 25 cts.   Real, 12 cts.

Real, 12 cts.   ½ Real, 6 cts.   ¼ Real, 3 cts.   ¼ Real, 3 cts.   ¼ Real, 3 cts.   ¼ Real, 6 cts   ¼ Real, 6 cts

GOLD COINS OF SOUTH AND CENTRAL AMERICA.

Old Doubloon, $15.50.   Old Doubloon, $15.50.   Doubloon, $15.50.   Doubloon, $15.50.

Doubloon, $15.50.   Doubloon, $15.50.   Doubloon, $15.50.   Doubloon, $15.50.

GOLD COINS OF SOUTH AND CENTRAL AMERICA—*Continued.*

Doubloon, $15.50.   Doubloon, $15.50.   Doubloon $15.50.   Doubloon $15.50

Doubloon, $15.50.   Doubloon, $15.25.   ½ Doubloon, $7.75.   ½ Doubloon, $7.75.   Moidore, $6.

½ Pistole, $1.87.   ½ Pistole, $1.75.   Doubloon, $15.50.   Doubloon, $15.50.   ½ Pistole, $1.87.   ½ Pistole, $1.87.

½ Joe, (Brazil) $8 to $8.50.   Moidore, (Brazil) $4.75.   Moidore, $4.75.   ½ Doubloon, $3.07.   Pistole, $4.75.   Pistole, $4.75.

Pistole, $3.75.   Pistole, $3.75.   Pistole, $3.75.   Pistole, $3.75.   Pistole, $4.50.   ½ Doubloon, $1.90.   ½ Pistole, $1.87.

½ Pistole, 90 cts.   ½ Pistole, 87 cts.   ½ Pistole, 90 cts.   ½ Pistole, 90 cts.   ½ Pistole, 90 cts.   ½ Pistole, (Brazil) 90 cts.   ½ Pistole, $1.87.   ½ Pistole, $1.87

SILVER COINS OF SOUTH AND CENTRAL AMERICA.

900 Reis, $1.

900 Reis, $1.

960 Reis, $1.

Piece of 1200, $1.

960 Reis, $1.

Eight reals, $1.

Eight reals, $1.

Eight reals, $1.

Eight reals, $1.

Eight reals, $1.

Eight reals, $1.

Eight reals, $1.

Eight reals, $1.

Eight reals, $1.

Eight reals, $1.

Eight reals, $1.

Eight reals, $1.

Eight reals, $1.

Eight reals, $1.

Eight reals, $1.

SILVER COINS OF SOUTH AND CENTRAL AMERICA—*Continued.*

Eight reals, 97 cts.   Eight reals, 97 cts.   Eight reals, 97 cts.   Eight reals, 97 cts.

Eight reals, 97 cts.   Eight reals, $1.05.   Eight reals, 96 cts.   Eight reals, 57 cts.

Patagon, 90 cts.   Eight reals, (base) 60 cts.   Eight reals, (base) 60 cts.   Eight reals (base) 60 cts.

50 cts.   Four reals. 45 cts.   Four reals. 45 cts.   300 Reis, 25 cts.

Four reals, 45 cts.   Four reals, 45 cts.   Four reals, 45 cts.   Four reals, 45 cts.

Real, 11 cts.   Real, 11 cts.   Real, 7 cts.   Real, 11 cts.   Real, 7 cts.   Real, 11 cts   Real, 11 cts

SILVER COINS OF SOUTH AND CENTRAL AMERICA—*Continued.*

| Four reals, 44 cts. | Four reals, 34 cts. | Four reals, (base) 33 cts. | Four reals, (base) 33 cts. | 2 Reals, 20 cts. |

| Two reals, 20 cts. | Two reals, 20 cts. | Two reals, 20 cts. | Two reals, 20 cts. | Two reals, 20 cts. |

| Two reals, 20 cts | Two reals, 20 cts. | Two reals, 20 cts. | Two reals, 20 cts. | Two reals, 20 cts. |

| Two reals, 20 cts. | Two reals, 20 cts. | Two reals, 20 cts. | Two reals, 20 cts | Two reals, 20 cts. |

| Two reals 20 cts. | Two reals, 20 cts. | Two reals, 20 cts. | Two reals, (base) 16 cts. | Two reals, (base) 16 cts. |

| Two reals, 15 cts. | Two reals, 15 cts. | Two reals, 15 cts | Two reals, 15 cts. | Two reals, 15 cts. | Two reals, 15 cts. |

     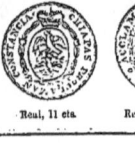 

| Real, 11 cts. | Real, 11 cts. | Real, 11 cts. | Real, 11 cts. | Real, 11 cts. | Real, 11 cts. | Real, 11 cts. |

SILVER COINS OF SOUTH AND CENTRAL AMERICA—*Continued.*

Real, 10 cts.	Real, 10 cts.	Real, 10 cts.	Real, 10 cts.	Real, 10 cts.	Real, 10 cts.	Real, 10 cts.
Real, 10 cts.	Real, 10 cts.	Real, 10 cts.	Real, 10 cts.	Real, 10 cts.	Real, 10 cts.	Real, 10 cts.
Real, 10 cts.	Real, 10 cts.	Real, 10 cts.	Real, 10 cts.	Real, 8 cts.	Real, 8 cts.	Real, 8 cts.
Real, 8 cts.	Real, 6 cts.	Real, 5 cts.	Real, 5 cts.	½ Real, 5 cts	½ Real, 4 cts.	½ Real, 5 cts.	½ Real, 5 cts.

½ Real, 5 cts.   ½ Real, 5 cts.   ½ Real, 5 cts.   ½ Real, 5 cts.   ½ Real, 5 cts.

GOLD COINS OF GREAT BRITAIN.

Double Sovereign, $9.64.	Mohur, $6.72.	5 Sovereigns, $24.10.	Guinea, $5.	Guinea, $5.
½ Guinea, $2.50.	½ Guinea, $2.50.	Sovereign, $4.82.	Sovereign, $4.82.	Sovereign, $4.82.	Sovereign, $4.82.	Sovereign, $4.82.
½ Guinea, $1.66.	¼ Sovereign, $2.40.	¼ Guinea, $2.50.	¼ Sovereign, $2.40.	¼ Sovereign, $2.30.	¼ Sovereign, $2.40.	¼ Sovereign, $2.40.	¼ Sovereign, $2.40.

SILVER COINS OF GREAT BRITAIN.

William III. crown, $1.10.　　William III. crown, $1.10.　　Queen Anne crown, $1.10.　　Queen Anne crown, $1.10.

Victoria crown, $1.10.　　Victoria crown, $1.10.　　George III. crown, $1.10.　　Victoria crown, $1.10.

Bank of Ireland 6s. token, $4.　　Bank of Ireland 6s. token, $1.　　Crown, $1　　Charles II. crown, $1.10.

Bank of England 4s. token, $1.　　William and Mary ½ crown, 55 cts.　　William and Mary ½ crown, 55 cts.　　William and Mary ½ crown, 55 cts.

Queen Anne ½ crown, 55 cts.　　Charles II. ½ crown, 55 cts.　　½ Crown, 55 cts.　　½ Crown, 55 cts.

SILVER COINS OF GREAT BRITAIN—*Continued.*

George IV. ½ crown, 55 cts.   ½ Crown, 55 cts.   ½ Crown, 55 cts.   ½ Crown, 55 cts.   Victoria ½ crown, 55 cts.

Charles II. ½ crown, 55 cts.   George III. ½ crown, 55 cts.   William & Mary ½ crown, 55 cts.   ½ Crown, 55 cts.   Queen Anne ½ crown, 55 cts.

½ Crown, 55 cts.   Three shillings token, 50 cts.   Three shillings token, 50 cts.   One-and-sixpenny token, 22 cts

Irish 30-penny token, 40 cts   Victoria florin, 45 cts.   Victoria florin, 45 cts.   Thirty-penny shinplaster, 40 cts.   Thirty-penny shinplaster, 40 cts.

One-and-sixpenny token, 22 cts.   Shilling, 22 cts.   Shilling, 22 cts   Shilling, 22 cts.   Shilling, 22 cts   Shilling, 22 cts.

Shilling, 22 cts.   Shilling, 22 cts.   Sixpence of Queen Elizabeth, 11 cts   11 cts.

Sixpence, 11 cts.   Sixpence, 11 cts.   Sixpence, 11 cts.   Sixpence, 11 cts.   Sixpence, 11 cts.   Sixpence, 11 cts.

SILVER COINS OF GREAT BRITAIN—*Continued.*

Fourpence, 7 cts. Fourpence, 7 cts. 4d, 7 cts. Fourpenny Piece, 7 cts. Sixpenny Token, 6 cts.

Threepenny Piece, 5 cts. Threepenny piece, 5 cts. Threepenny Piece, 5 cts. Twopenny Piece, 3 cts.

Twopenny Piece, 3 cts. 1½d, 2 cts. 1d, 2 cts.

COLONIAL SILVER COINS OF GREAT BRITAIN.

Dollar, or ten macutes, 80 cts. Dollar, or ten macutes, 80 cts. Three gilders, 73 cts. Rupee, 40 cts.

Rupee, 40 cts. Rupee, 40 cts. Rupee, 40 cts. Rupee, 40 cts. Rupee, 40 cts.

½ Pagoda, 34 cts. ¼ Dollar, 22 cts. Shilling, 22 cts. ¼ Rupee, 20 cts. ½ Rupee, 20 cts. Two macutes, 20 cts.

¼ Gilder, 12 cts. ½ Gilder, 12 cts. 11 cts. 11 cts. ¼ Rupee, 10 cts. ¼ Rupee, 10 cts.

½ Gilder, 6 cts. 2 Annas, 5 cts. ⅛ Rupee, 10 cts. 5 cts. ¼ Gilder, 3 cts.

GOLD COINS OF FRANCE.

Double Louis-d'or, $9.　　40 francs, $7.64.　　40 francs, $7.64.　　40 francs, $7.64.

Louis-d'or, $4.50.　　Louis-d'or, $4.50.　　20 Francs, $3.82.　　20 Francs, $3.82.　　20 Francs, $3.82.　　40 Francs, $7.64.

20 Francs, $3.82.　　20 Francs, $3.82.　　20 Francs, $3.82.　　10 Francs, $1.53.　　6 Francs, $1.10.

SILVER COINS OF FRANCE.

Crown, $1.　　Crown, $1.　　Crown, $1.　　Crown, $1.

Six francs, $1.　　Six francs, $1　　Six livres, $1.06.　　Five francs, 90 cts.

Five francs, 90 cts.　　Five francs, 90 cts.　　Five francs, 90 cts.　　Five francs, 90 cts.

SILVER COINS OF FRANCE—*Continued.*

Five francs, 90 cts.   Five francs, 90 cts.   Five francs, 90 cts.   Five francs, 90 cts.

Five francs, 90 cts.   Five francs, 90 cts.   Five francs, 90 cts.   Five francs, 90 cts.

¼ Crown, 50 cts.   Five francs, 90 cts.   Five francs, 90 cts.   ½ Crown, 50 cts.

Two francs, 36 cts.   Two francs, 36 cts.   ¼ Crown, 24 cts.   30 Sols, 24 cts.

20 Sols, 15 cts.   30 Sols, 24 cts.   30 Sols, 24 cts.   24 cts.   15 Sols, 12 cts.

Franc, 18 cts.   Franc, 18 cts.   ¼ Crown, 12 cts.   ¼ Crown, 12 cts.   ¼ Crown, 12 cts.   12 Sols, 10 cts.

SILVER COINS OF FRANCE—*Continued.*

¼ Crown, 12 cts.	6 cts.	8 cts.	1-16 Crown, 6 cts.	1-16 Crown, 8 cts.	10 Sols, 3 cts.	25 Centimes, 4 cts.

10 Sols, 8 cts.	½ Franc, 8 cts.	½ Franc, 8 cts.	½ Franc, 8 cts.	50 Centimes, 8 cts.	25 Centimes, 4 cts.	¼ Franc, 4 cts.	¼ Franc, 4 cts.

GOLD COINS OF SPAIN.

¼ Pistole, $2

Doubloon, $15.57.	Quarter Doubloon, $4.	Pistole, $4.	Pistole, $4.	¼ Pistole, $2.	¼ Pistole, $1. ¼ Pistole, $1.

SILVER COINS OF SPAIN.

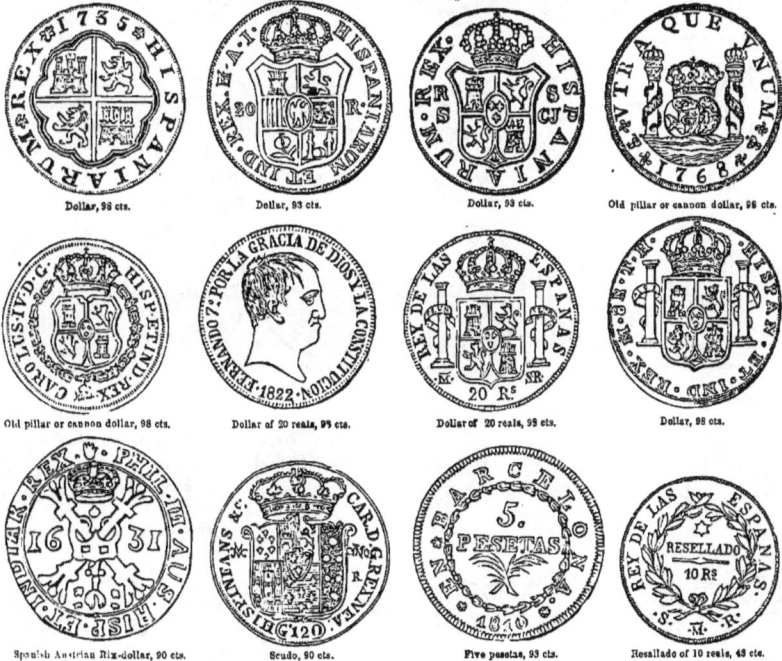

Dollar, 98 cts.	Dollar, 93 cts.	Dollar, 93 cts.	Old pillar or cannon dollar, 96 cts.

Old pillar or cannon dollar, 98 cts.	Dollar of 20 reals, 95 cts.	Dollar of 20 reals, 99 cts.	Dollar, 98 cts.

Spanish Austrian Rix-dollar, 90 cts.	Scudo, 90 cts.	Five pesetas, 93 cts.	Resallado of 10 reals, 48 cts.

SILVER COINS OF SPAIN—*Continued.*

½ Dollar, 48 cts.   ½ Dollar, 48 cts.   ½ Dollar, 45 cts.   ½ Dollar, 45 cts.   ½ Dollar, (pillar) 45 cts.

Double pistareen, 36 cts.   Double pistareen, 36 cts.   ½ Dollar, 20 cts.   ½ Dollar, 20 cts.   ½ Dollar, 20 cts.

½ Dollar, 22 cts.   Pillar ½ Dollar, 22 cts.   Quarter Dollar, 22 cts.   ½ Dollar, 20 cts.   Head pistareen, 16 cts.   Head pistareen, 16 cts.

Pistareen, 16 cts.   Pistareen, 16 cts.   Pistareen, 16 cts.   Pistareen, 16 cts.   Pistareen, 16 cts.   Pistareen, 16 cts.

Pistareen, 16 cts.   Peseta, 16 cts.   Peseta 16 cts.   Pistareen, 16 cts.   Pistareen, 16 cts.   Pistareen, 16 cts.

Pistareen, 16 cts.   Pistareen, 16 cts.   Medio, 10 cts.   Medio, 10 cts.   ½ Pistareen, 7 cts.   ½ Pistareen, 7 cts

½ Pistareen, 7 cts.   ½ Medio, 5 cts.   ½ Medio, 5 cts.   ½ Pistareen, 4 cts.   ½ Pistareen, 4 cts.

GOLD COINS OF PORTUGAL AND BRAZIL.

Moidore, $4.75.   Moidore, $6.   Dobrao, $34.   ½ Joe, $6 to $8.50.   Crown, $5.75.

50 cts.   75 cts. $1.75.   20 cts   50 cts.   60 cts.

SILVER COINS OF PORTUGAL AND BRAZIL.

960 Reis, 98 cts.   960 Reis, 98 cts.   960 Reis, 98 cts.   960 Reis, 98 cts.

Piece of 1200 Reis, 95 cts.   960 Reis, 98 cts.   960 Reis, 98 cts.   Piece of 1200 Reis, 98 cts.

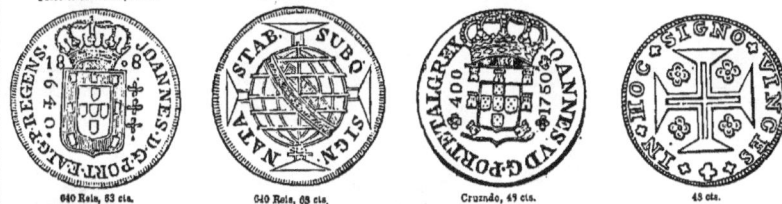

640 Reis, 53 cts.   640 Reis, 63 cts.   Cruzado, 49 cts.   45 cts.

½ Crown 48 cts.   ¼ Crown, 46 cts.   300 Reis, 35 cts.   Piece of 200 Reis, 20 cts.

SILVER COINS OF PORTUGAL AND BRAZIL—*Continued.*

200 Reis, 15 cts.   150 Reis, 14 cts.   150 Reis, 14 cts.   90 Reis, 10 cts.   Piece of 60 Reis, 10 cts.   Piece of 60 Reis, 10 cts.

40 Reis, 5 cts.   40 Reis, 5 cts.   40 Reis, 5 cts.   40 Reis, 5 cts.   40 Reis, 5 cts.

GOLD AND SILVER COINS OF SWITZERLAND.

Crown of Zurich, 96 cts.   Crown of Geneva, 96 cts.   4 Francs, 96 cts.   4 Francs 96 cts.

4 Francs, 96 cts.   4 Francs, 96 cts.   2 Francs, 48 cts.   2 Francs, 48 cts.

10½ Batzen, 22 cts.   5 Livres, 90 cts.   10 Batzen, 18 cts.   10 Batzen, 20 cts.

10 Batzen, 18 cts.   10 Batzen, 18 cts.   20 Schillings, 10 cts.   5 Batzen, 8 cts.   5 Batzen, 8 cts.

SILVER AND GOLD COINS OF SWITZERLAND—*Continued.*

5 Batzen, 3 cts.　　5 Batzen, 3 cts.　　5 Batzen, 3 cts.　　5 Batzen, 3 cts.　　25 Centimes, 3 cts.

Ducat, (Gold) $2 20.　　　　　　　2½ Batzen, 3 cts.

GOLD AND SILVER COINS OF AUSTRIA AND HUNGARY.

Quadruple Ducat, (Gold) $8.75.　　Three marks, (Silver) $1.10.　　Crown of Brabant, (Silver) $1.

Soverain, (Gold) $6.66.　Soverain, (Gold) $6.63.　Soverain, (Gold) $6.63.　Soverain, (Gold) $6.63.　Double Ducat, (Gold) $4.75.　½ Sov., (Gold) $3.32.

½ Sov., (Gold) $3.32.　½ Sov., (Gold) $3.32.　½ Sov., Gold) $3.32.　Ducat, (Gold) $2.25.　Ducat, (Gold) $2.25.　Ducat, (Gold) $2.25.　Ducat, (Gold) $2.25.

Austrian Rix-dollar, (Silver) 90 cts.　Rix-dollar, (Silver) 90 cts.　Imperial Dollar, (Silver) 90 cts.

SILVER COINS OF AUSTRIA AND HUNGARY—*Continued.*

Austrian Rix-dollar, 90 cts.   Rix-dollar, 90 cts.   Rix-dollar, 90 cts.

Hungary Rix-dollar, 90 cts.   Florin, 38 cts   Florin, 38 cts.

Hungarian Dollar, 90 cts.   78 cts.   78 cts.

Thaler, 64 cts.   Thaler, 64 cts.   Thaler, 64 cts.   ½ Rix-dollar, 43 cts.

½ Crown, 50 cts.   Two marks, 50 cts.   Hungarian ½ Dollar, 45 cts   Mark, 30 cts.

SILVER AND GOLD COINS OF AUSTRIA AND HUNGARY—*Continued:*

Two lire, 20 cts.   ¼ Rix-dollar, 21 cts.   ½ Florin, 20 cts.   Third of a thaler, 20 cts.   30 Kreutzers, 20 cts.

¼ Florin, 16 cts.   20 Kreutzers, 14 cts.   20 Kreutzers, 14 cts.   ¼ Mark, 11 cts.   Eight Schilling, 11 cts.

¼ Mark, 11 cts.   Ducat, (Gold) $2.21.   10 Kreutzers, 6 cts.   5 Kreutzers, 3 cts.   5 Kreutzers, 3 cts

GOLD AND SILVER COINS OF THE GERMAN STATES.

Quintuple Ducat, $11.   Quintuple Ducat, $11.   Double thaler, (Silver) $1.30.   Double thaler, (Silver) $1.30.

10 Thaler, $7.86.   Double Fred. d'or $7.88.   Double Christ'n d'or, $7.86.   10 Thaler, $7.86.   10 Thaler, $7.88.

10 Thaler, $7.86.   Double Fred. d'or, $7.86.   10 Thaler, $7.86.   Double Fred. d'or, $7.80.   10 Thaler, $7.86.

GOLD COINS OF THE GERMAN STATES—*Continued.*

10 Thaler, $7.86.   10 Thaler, $7.86.   10 Thaler, $7.86.   Carolin, $4.80.   Carolin, $4.80.

Carolin, $4.80.   25 Francs, $4.75.   Double Ducat, $4.50.   Double Ducat, $4.50.   10 Gilders, $4.   10 Gilders, $4.

5 Thaler, $3.90.   5 Thaler, $3.90.   Thaler, $3.90.   Fred. d'or, $3.90.   5 Thaler, $3.90.   5 Thaler, $3.90.

5 Thaler, $3.90.   5 Thaler, 3.90.   5 Thaler, $3.90.   5 Thaler, $3.96.   5 Thaler, $3.96.

5 Thaler, $3.90.   5 Thaler, $3.90.   ½ Carolin, $2.40.   ½ Carolin, $2.40.   ½ Carolin, $2.35.   Ducat, $2.20.   Ducat, $2.20.

Ducat, $2.20.   Ducat, $2.20.   Ducat, $2.20.   Ducat, $2.20.   Ducat, $2.20.   Ducat, $2.20.   Ducat, $2.20.

Ducat, $2.20.   Ducat, $2.20.   Ducat, $2.20.   5 Gilders, $1.98.   5 Gilders, $1.98.   5 Gilders, $1.98.   2½ Thaler, $1.95.

10 Francs, $1.90.   10 Francs, $1.90.   12 Marks, $1.53.   ¼ Carolin, $1.18.   24 cts.

SILVER COINS OF THE GERMAN STATES—*Continued.*

Double thaler, $1.30.

Double thaler, $1.30.

Double thaler $1.30

Double thaler, $1.30.

Double thaler, $1.30.

Double thaler, $1 30.

Double thaler, $1.30.

Double thaler, $1.30.

Three gilders, $1.06.

Crown thaler, $1.

$1.

Crown, $1.

Specie thaler, $1.

Crown of Baden, $1.

Crown of Baden, $1.

Crown thaler, $1.

Crown thaler, $1.

Crown Thaler, $1.

Crown thaler, $1.

Crown thaler, $1.

SILVER COINS OF THE GERMAN STATES—*Continued.*

Wurtemburgh crown, $1.

Wurtemburgh crown, $1.

Old crown, 90 cts.

Convention thaler, 90 cts.

Rix-dollar, 90 cts.

Convention thaler, 90 cts.

Rix-dollar, 90 cts.

Rix-dollar, 90 cts.

6 Marks, 90 cts.

Rix-dollar, 90 cts.

Specie thaler, 90 cts.

Specie thaler, 90 cts.

Specie thaler, 90 cts.

Specie dollar of Bavaria, 90 cts.

Specie dollar of Bavaria, 90 cts.

Convention thaler, 90 cts.

Convention thaler, 90 cts.

Convention thaler, 90 cts.

Convention thaler, 90 cts.

Convention thaler, 90 cts.

SILVER COINS OF THE GERMAN STATES—*Continued.*

Convention thaler, 90 cts.   Convention thaler, 90 cts.   Convention thaler, 90 cts.   Convention thaler, 90 cts.

Convention thaler, 90 cts.   Convention thaler, 90 cts.   Convention thaler, 90 cts.   Convention thaler, 90 cts.

Rix-dollar, 90 cts.   Rix-dollar, 90 cts.   Rix-dollar, 90 cts.   Rix-dollar, 90 cts.

Specie-dollar of Bavaria, 90 cts.   Convention thaler, 90 cts.   90 cts.   5 Livres, 90 cts.

2½ Gilders, 90 cts.   Four marks, 80 cts.   Four marks, 80 cts.   Double gilder, 76 cts.

SILVER COINS OF THE GERMAN STATES—*Continued.*

Two gilders. 70 cts. | 70 cts. | Double gilder, 70 cts. | Thaler, 70 cts.

Thaler, 65 cts. | Thaler, 65 cts | Thaler, 65 cts | Thaler, 65 cts.

Thaler, 65 cts. | Thaler, 65 cts. | Thaler, 65 cts. | Thaler, 65 cts.

Thaler, 65 cts. | Thaler, 65 cts. | Thaler, 65 cts. | Thaler, 65 cts

Thaler, 65 cts. | Thaler, 65 cts. | Thaler, 65 cts. | Thaler, 65 cts.

2 cts. | 2 cts. | 3 Kreutzers, 2 cts. | 6 Pfennigs, 1 ct. | 6 Pfennigs, 1 ct. | 1 ct.

SILVER COINS OF THE GERMAN STATES—*Continued.*

Thaler, 65 cts.

Thaler, 65 cts.

Two marks, 50 cts.

Two marks, 50 cts.

Two marks, 50 cts.

Florin, 45 cts.

Florin, 45 cts.

Two marks, 50 cts.

Hungarian ½ dollar, 45 cts.

24 Mar. groschen, 45 cts.

½ Specie thaler, 45 cts.

Florin, 42 cts.

Florin, 42 cts.

Florin, 42 cts.

Florin, 42 cts.

Florin, 42 cts.

Florin, 42 cts.

Florin, 42 cts.

Florin, 42 cts.

Florin, 42 cts.

Florin, 42 cts.

Florin, 42 cts.

Florin, 42 cts.

SILVER COINS OF THE GERMAN STATES—*Continued.*

½ Specie thaler, 42 cts.   Florin, 42 cts.   ⅓ Specie thaler, 42 cts.   Florin, 36 cts.

Florin, 28 cts.   Florin, 35 cts.   Florin, 38 cts.   Florin, 33 cts.

Florin, 38 cts.   2½ Francs, 37 cts.   2½ Francs, 37 cts.   Florin, 35 cts.   Gilder, 35 cts.

Gilder, 35 cts.   Gilder, 35 cts.   Mark, 25 cts.   36 Grotes 28 cts.   One-third piece, 28 cts.

½ Thaler, 30 cts.   Two lire, 30 cts.   1-6 Rix-dollar, 20 cts.   30 Kreutzers, 20 cts.   ½ Florin, 20 cts.

½ Florin, 20 cts.   ½ Thaler, 20 cts.   ½ Florin, 20 cts.   ⅓ Florin, 20 cts.   ½ Florin, 20 cts.

SILVER COINS OF THE GERMAN STATES—*Continued.*

½ Florin, 20 cts.   ⅓ of a Thaler, 20 cts.   ⅓ Florin, 20 cts.   ⅓ of a Thaler, 20 cts.   ½ Gilder, 16 cts.

10 Schilling, 15 cts.   20 Kreutzers, 15 cts.   20 Kreutzers, 15 cts.   20 Kreutzers, 15 cts.

20 Kreutzers, 15 cts.   20 Kreutzers, 15 cts.   20 Kreutzers, 15 cts.   20 Schillings, (base) 12 cts.

½ Gilder, 17 cts.   ½ Gilder, 17 cts.   1-6 Specie thaler, 15 cts.   1-6 Specie thaler, 15 cts.   20 Grani, 15 cts.   6 Marien groschen, 12 cts.

20 Schillings, 12 cts.   6 Marien groschen, 12 cts.   ⅓ Mark, 12 cts.   1-6 Thaler, 10 cts.   ⅓ Florin, 10 cts.   1-6 Thaler, 10 cts.

1-6 Thaler, 10 cts.   ½ Florin, 10 cts.   12 Grotes, 10 cts.   12 Grotes, 10 cts.   ½ Florin, 10 cts.   1-6 Thaler, 10 cts.

12 Grotes, 10 cts.   10 cts.   1-6 Thaler, 10 cts.   1-6 Piece, 10 cts   1-6 Piece, 10 cts.   1-6 Piece, 10 cts.

SILVER COINS OF THE GERMAN STATES—*Continued.*

1-6 Thaler, 10 cts.   1-6 Thaler, 10 cts.   1-6 Pieces, 10 cts.   1-6 Thaler, 8 cts.   1-6 Thaler, 8 cts.   ¼ Gilder, 8 cts.

4 Marien groschen, 8 cts.   4 Marien groschen, 8 cts.   5 Schillings, 8 cts   25 Centimes 8 cts.   10 Kreutzers, 8 cts.

¼ Mark, 6 cts.   ¼ Mark, 6 cts.   1-12 Thaler, 6 cts.   Six grotes, 5 cts.   Six grotes, 5 cts.   1-12 Piece, 5 cts.

1 ct.   4 cts.   4 cts.   4 cts.   Lira, 4 cts.   10 Centimes, 4 cts.   5 Centimes, 2 cts

6 Kreutzers, 3 cts.   6 Kreutzers, 3 cts.   6 Kreutzers, 3 cts.   Two groschen, 2 cts.   24th of a Thaler, 2 cts.   Two groschen, 2 cts.   1 ct.

GOLD COINS OF ITALY.

80 Livres, $15.30.   100 Livres, $19.15.   96 Livres, $15.   96 Livres, $15.

96 Livres, $15.   10 Scudi, $10.   40 Livres, $7.60.   40 Livres, $7.60.   40 Livres, $7.60.

GOLD COINS OF ITALY—*Continued.*

40 Livres, $7.00.   2 Doppia, $6.25.   2 Doppia, $6.25.   20 Livres, $3.50.   20 Livres, $3.50.   6 Drachm, $5.50.

20 Livres, $3.50.   20 Livres, $3.50.   20 Livres, $3.50.   20 Livres, $3.50.   Sequin, $2.20.   10 Livres, $1.90.

SILVER COINS OF ITALY.

Ten livres of Tuscany, $1.50.   Ten livres of Tuscany, $1.50.   Sardinian scudo, $1.25.

Sardinian scudo, $1.25.   Ten pauls of Tuscany, 95 cts.   Roman crown, 95 cts.

Ten pauls, 95 cts.   Ten pauls of Tuscany, 95 cts.   Roman scudo, 95 cts.   Crown of Bologna, 95 cts.

SILVER COINS OF ITALY—*Continued.*

Venetian scudo, 95 cts.   Crown of Bologna, 95 cts.   Scudo, 90 cts.   Sicilian scudo, 90 cts.

Sicilian scudo, 90 cts.   Sicilian scudo, 90 cts.   Scudo, 90 cts.   Scudo, 90 cts.

Scudo, 90 cts.   Scudo, 90 cts.   Scudo, 90 cts.   Roman scudo, 95 cts.

Scudo, 90 cts.   Scudo, 90 cts.   Five lire of Lombardy, 90 cts.   Five lire of Lombardy, 90 cts.

Five livres, 90 cts.   Five livres, 90 cts.   Five livres, 90 cts.   Five livres, 90 cts.

SILVER COINS OF ITALY—*Continued.*

Five francs, 90 cts.

Five lire, 90 cts.

Five francs, 90 cts.

Five francs, 90 cts.

Five francs, 90 cts.

Neapolitan scudo, 54 cts.

5 Drachms. (Greece) 78 cts.

Neapolitan silver ducat, 72 cts.

¼ Scudo, 45 cts.

½ Scudo, 46 cts.

¼ Scudo, 45 cts.

¼ Scudo, 45 cts.

¼ Scudo, 44 cts.

Five pauls, 44 cts.

Five pauls, 44 cts.

Fifty grani, 36 cts.

Fifty grani, 36 cts.

Two livres, 35 cts.

Two livres, 35 cts.

Two livres, 35 cts.

¼ Scudo, 23 cts.

Roman scudo, 28 cts.

Roman testoon, 28 cts.

Two lire, 35 cts.

Two lire, 35 cts.

Two lire of Sicily, 35 cts.

SILVER COINS OF ITALY—*Continued.*

Two lire of Sicily, 35 cts.   Roman testoon, 28 cts.   Roman testoon, 25 cts.   Roman testoon, 28 cts.   Roman testoon, 28 cts.   Two pauls, 18 cts.

Florin, 18 cts.   Lira 18 cts.   1-5th Scudo of Lucca, 18 cts.   1-5 Scudo of Lucca, 18 cts.   Sicilian liva, 16 cts.   Sicilian lira, 16 cts.

Franc, 16 cts.   Livre, 16 cts.   Drachme, (Greece) 15 cts.   20 Grani, 15 cts.   Two carlin, 15 cts.   20 Grani, 15 cts.

20 Grani, 15 cts.   Two carlin, 15 cts.   20 Grani, 15 cts.   Two carlin, 15 cts.   ½ Testoon, 14 cts.   ½ Testoon, 14 cts.

½ Drachme, (Greece) 7 cts.   10 Soldi, 7 cts.   ½ Testoon, 7 cts.   Paul, 7 cts.   10 Soldi, 7 cts.   10 Soldi, 7 cts.   50 Centimes, 7 cts.

6 cts.   10 Grani, 6 cts.   6 cts.   Carlin, 6 cts.   6 cts.   6 cts.   5 Soldi, 4 cts.   5 Soldi, 4 cts.

SILVER COINS OF SWEDEN, DENMARK, AND NORWAY.

Specie dollar, 85 cts.   8 Marks, $1.10.   Marks, $1.10.   Specie dollar, 98 cts.

SILVER COINS OF SWEDEN, DENMARK, AND NORWAY—*Continued.*

Specie dollar, 98 cts. Old ducatoon, 90 cts. Old ducatoon, 90 cts. Rix-dollar 98 cts.

40 Schillings, 60 cts. 73 cts. 73 cts. 4 Marks, 48 cts.

½ Specie dollar, 44 cts. 4 Marks, 48 cts. 4 Marks, 48 cts. ½ Specie dollar, 44 cts.

16 Skillings, (base) 10 cts. ½ Rix-dollar, 48 cts. 1-5 Specie dollar, (base) 25 cts. 12 Skillings, (base) 10 cts.

24 Skillings, 10 cts. ¼ Specie dollar, 29 cts. ¼ Specie dollar, 20 cts. 12 Skillings, (base) 10 cts. 20 Skillings, 5 cts. 20 Skillings, 5 cts.

GOLD & SILVER COINS OF SWEDEN, DENMARK, AND NORWAY.

Double Ducat, (Sweden) Gold, $4.40.   6 Skillings, 8 cts.   24 Skillings, 6 cts.   2 Skillings, 4 cts   8 Skillings, 4 cts.   5 cts.

3 cts.   3 cts.   2 cts.   1 ct.   1 ct.   1 ct.

SILVER COINS OF NETHERLANDS AND HOLLAND.

Silver lion, 98.   3 Gilders, $1.06.   Old Rix-dollar, 98 cts.   Silver lion, 98 cts.

60 Schillings, 98 cts.   Crown of Zurich, 98 cts.   Ducatoon, 90 cts.   Specie dollar, 98 cts.

⅔ Rix-dollar, 60 cts.   Ducatoon, 90 cts.   Rix-dollar, 90 cts.   30 Stivers, 23 cts

SILVER COINS OF NETHERLANDS AND HOLLAND—*Continued.*

Rix-dollar, 90 cts. Rix-dollar, 90 cts. Rix-dollar, 90 cts. Rix-dollar, 90 cts.

Specie dollar, 94 cts. Old Rix-dollar, 90 cts. ½ Rix-dollar, 38 cts. ½ Rix-dollar, 38 cts.

2 Stivers, 3 cts. 30 Stivers, 56 cts. Rix-dollar, 90 cts. ½ Thaler, 43 cts. 2 Stivers, 3 cts.

Gilder, 30 cts. 10 Stivers, 18 cts. Gilder, 34 cts. Gilder, 34 cts. 10 Stivers, 18 cts.

8 cts. 7 Stivers, 9 cts. 8 Stivers, 6 cts. 1-6 Rix-dollar, 15 cts. 6 Stivers, 9 cts. 6 Stivers, 6 cts.

GOLD AND SILVER COINS OF RUSSIA AND POLAND.

5 Roubles, (Gold) $3.95.   5 Roubles, (Gold) $3.90.   Imperial, (Gold) $4.

Rouble and a half, $1.07.   Rouble, 75 cts.   Rouble, 76 cts.   Rouble, 78 cts.

Rouble, 75 cts.   Rouble, 78 cts.   Rouble, 78 cts.   Rouble, 78 cts.

5 Zlot, 50 cts.   5 Zlot, 50 cts.   5 Zlot, 48 cts.   5 Zlot, 48 cts.   ½ Roub. , 34 cts.

½ Rouble, 35 cts.   ½ Rouble, 35 cts.   ½ Rouble, 34 cts.   2 Zlot, 18 cts.   30 Kopeks, 18 cts.

25 Kopeks, 13 cts.   25 Kopeks, 13 cts.   1 Zl t, 10 cts.   20 Kopeks, 10 cts.   10 Kopeks, 5 cts.   10 Kopeks, 5 cts.   5 Kopeks, 3 cts.

SILVER AND GOLD COINS OF TURKEY.

20 Piastres, 86 cts.　　20 Piastres, 86 cts.　　20 Piastres, 86 cts.　　5 Drachmi, 90 cts.

Utchlik, 10 cts　　¼ Altilik, 10 cts　　Altmichlik, 5 cts　　Piastre, 4 cts

20 Drachmi, (Gold) $3.40.　　¼ Drachm, 8 cts.

SILVER COINS OF HAYTI.

The genuine pieces of Hayti are of low silver, and a large number of those in circulation are counterfeit, consequently no value is attached to them except as curiosities by antiquarians.

TRIPOLITAN AND JEWISH COINS.

A Jewish coin, 15 cts.　　Gherab of Tripoli, (Copper) 10 cts.　　3 cts.

SILVER COINS OF THE NETHERLANDS.

¼ Rix-dollar, 42 cts　　　　　¼ Florin, 10 cts.

SILVER COINS OF CANADA.

Ten-cent Piece, 10 cts.   Twenty-cent Piece, 20 cts.   Five-cent Piece, 5 cts.